ST PAUL'S
A PLACE TO DREAM

A new way of looking at
St Paul's Cathedral

Words

JOHN HENCHER & CHRISTOPHER HERBERT

Photographs

ANDREW TALBOT-PONSONBY

Published by
The Friends of St. Paul's

This Book is dedicated
with Her kind permission

to

HER MAJESTY QUEEN ELIZABETH THE QUEEN MOTHER

Patron of the Friends of Saint Paul's

with respect and affection

E
N
S
W

4

9 & 10
Way down
to Crypt

6

5

7

3

2

11
Way up to Dome
& Whispering Gallery

8

1

12

CONTENTS

INTRODUCTION

Welcome to St. Paul's Cathedral, one of the most famous buildings in the world. We have written this book to help you find your way around it, to discover its great riches and to look at it with fresh eyes.

Each section (and there are 12 in all) is devoted to a particular place in the Cathedral. We have called these places "Stations" for there you should stand, look around you and let your imagination run free. To help you to identify each Station there are photographs and at the front of the book a numbered map.

If you follow this guide you will go to some of the most important parts of the buildings and there, with the help of the readings, we hope you will discover more about yourself, more about the Cathedral and more about God.

Sir Christopher Wren

Station 1

At the Entrance to the Cathedral

This house of God replaced the one built from 1087 - 1240 which was destroyed by the fire of London in 1666. It was designed by Sir Christopher Wren and his epitaph reads, "If you would seek his monument look around you." You are standing at the West End of this great Cathedral, which was finished in 1708 and you should look around you with your eyes, with your imagination and with the knowledge that this is first of all a House of Prayer, built so that people may worship God in the name of Jesus.

God of the Way, teach me how to find you.

Christ in majesty

CHANGES

Doors close and light fades
And everything changed;
The high sky to a roof of shades,
Streets to pillars ranged
Along a path of stone.
Out there has all sound
Now turned to lowest tone,
Buses, cars and underground
Still near, but far away.
There we laughed and talked
On an outing day,
Then into stillness walked.
Now with this book in hand
And eyes that open wide,
Time to explore stranger land
Than the one we left outside.

IN THE BEGINNING

"In the beginning" he said "was the Word"

not dust
not planets
nor atoms
nor sunshine
just a Word
and ever since then
men have been searching
to speak it.

TIGER

"Ah" said the tiger, as he brushed around my legs, "but do you know why you have come here?"

"Of course I do" I replied. "I have come here to look at a famous building."

"A trick" said the tiger "a typical, human trick! You need to *sniff* buildings, not look at them.

"Sniff?"

"Yes. Sniff it, smell it; your nose should not be ignored. Go on" he commanded "sniff it."

I did as I was told.

"So....." he said, somewhat impatiently. "What can you smell?"

"Nothing much."

"You are completely and utterly useless" he retorted. "I can smell a thousand things here. Scents and spices from India, cherry blossom from Japan, snow from the Arctic ..." he seemed quite carried away.

"Sorry" I said "but I can't."

"Poor, poor creature" he said. "The whole world pours in through these doors. Stand here long enough and every nation on earth will pass by ... and what do they come for? I ask myself what do they come for?"

OPENING EYES

Almighty God, Creator of this beautiful world,
open our eyes to see your love at work so that
our lives may be a celebration of you.

Station 2

At the Font

You are standing by the Font. This great basin holds water in which people, usually as small babies, are baptised. To be baptised means to be christened; to be made a member of Christ's Church. Baptism is called a Sacrament, because it is one of the ways by which we are united to God, through Jesus.

WATER

When I was very young
An old man said to me,
Take care, all through your life,
Each and every day
Respect the power of WATER.

Washing my hands and face,
A long, hot bath in winter,
Turning on the taps,
Emptying the sink,
Releasing the flow of WATER.

Wet earth after the rain,
All the plants refreshed,
Trees drinking from their roots,
Enriching and reviving food,
Restored by the means of WATER.

Wide rivers and tiny streams
And ponds and reservoirs,
The locks, canals and springs,
Energy supplied by dams
Resisting the weight of WATER.

We need it for our thirst,
Approach its depth with care,
Tame it, save it, swim in it,
Embrace, enjoy and fear
Relentless might of WATER.

Wisdom of the Lord our God,
All praise to his name,
That we become his children,
Enter into His kingdom,
Reborn, baptised with WATER.

THE HOLY SPIRIT

Burst upon us, power of God,
Cleanse us, inspire us, strengthen us
that we may love you and love our neighbour
with all our hearts.

Thank you, Lord for water. Every day we drink it, wash in it, cook in it and use it in a hundred ways. Thank you for its purity and strength, its beauty and its grace. Without it we should die.
Lord, always give us water.

On the rails around the Font

The wetness and the clearness and the coldness.
The snowflake and icicle and hail and frost.
The fog, the raindrop, the dew and the cloud.
A cup of tea, a giass of milk, a swimming pool, an ocean and a font. Cooling towers and radiators, ice-rinks and waterfalls.
Water, water, water.

Station 3

Beneath the Dome

This dome is the second largest in the world; the largest is in St. Peter's in Rome. If you climb to the very top you will have to use 607 steps. On the way up you will go through the Whispering Gallery, where, when it is quiet, a whisper will travel right round the inside wall. From the Stone Gallery and the Golden Gallery you get wonderful views of London. This Cathedral stands in the heart of the city as a symbol of the presence of God.

The still centre

"If you come very close" said the angel, "and stay very still you will see things to amaze you. For this is a place of birth where new thoughts, new dreams, new prayers struggle into life; a place of rejoicing where people are happy and take their ease; a place of music where songs ripple the air; a place of sorrow where hearts ache and groan with grief; a place of majesty and pomp and grandeur; a place where God parts the air like a rock cleaves the waterfall and longs to be seen."

Picture God as .....

a boy blowing bubbles
made of purest, radiant light
that float silently through space
as planets, stars and suns

an artist with a brush
mixing subtle, wondrous colours
that are stroked with tender kindness
upon all living things

a man upon a cross
telling those who will hear
that the deepest life in all things
is the Word called Love.

Chess-board

Four leaves like tattered rooks
gusted from the tree-tops
by a fierce, autumnal wind.

Three cliffs like helpless pawns
battered by the cudgels
of a black and angry sea.

Two trees like martyred knights
tourtured in the furnace
of a raging forest-fire.

One cave like a humbled king
wounded by the laughter
of a cruel jeering crowd.

Whispers

Dearest God,
please listen to the deepest thoughts I have,
to my most secret joys
for they are the whispers from my soul.

Station 4

At the Chapel of Modern Martyrs

People still suffer and are killed because of their Christian faith. This is the chapel of Modern Martyrs and they are remembered here just as, throughout the Cathedral, many great men and women have their memorials.

WHERE ARE THEY?

Where are those, who have died?
Names carved in stone, written in books,
Are they really 'on the other side',
Kings and soldiers, saints and crooks?
Or are they as dead as their statues are,
Sculptured into stony stillness?
No sun at dawn, no evening star,
Tasteless, soundless, sightless.

Have they all gone for ever,
Slipped away into the past?
Stupid and wise, dim and clever,
Are they all the same at last?
Died at eighty or at seventeen,
Rich and famous, unknown or poor,
All now gone beyond death's door.

These questions now I ask
For all the people who are dead,
They have done their earthly task,
They were given their daily bread.
They were all as I am now
But where they are I cannot tell,
Yet I still believe somehow
For us and them, that all is well.

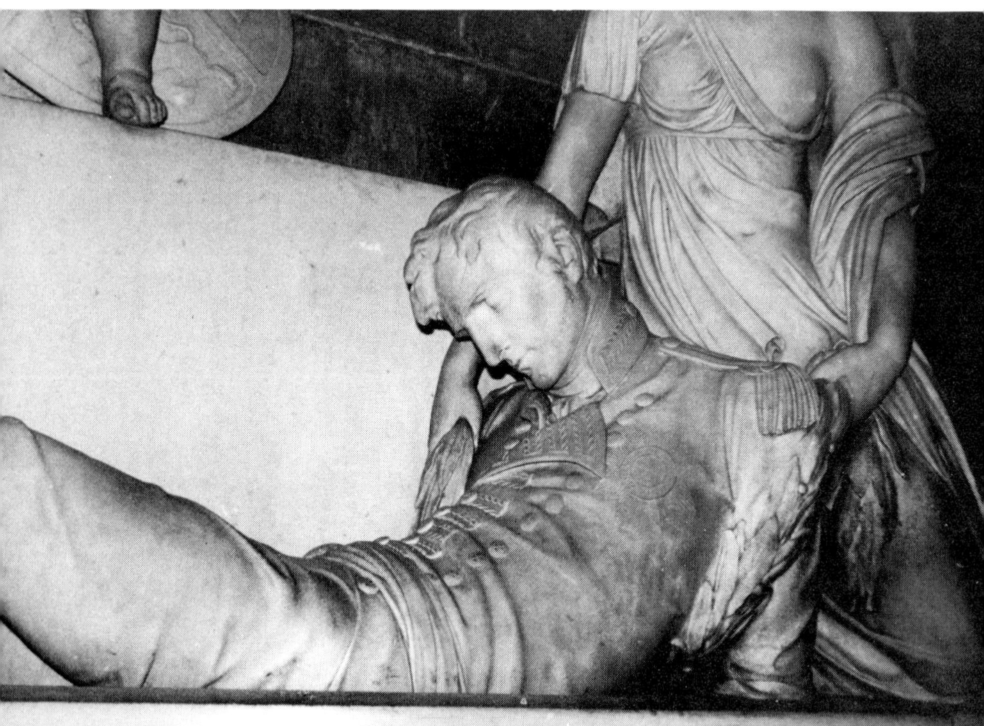

DEATH AND MEMORY

Each morning on his way to school, Richard saw the old lady sitting in her downstairs room. She always looked the same, her white hair soft against the dark red cushion, her cardigan neatly buttoned, her hands folded in her lap.

She sat facing down the road, as if she was waiting for someone to turn the corner. In the morning she didn't seem to notice Richard, but on his way home from school in the afternoon he saw her as soon as he turned the corner and as he reached the gate of the house next door she would lift up her right hand in greeting to him. Richard always paused, smiled, waved his hand and then broke into a run.

Every morning and every evening she was there, just the same, her chair drawn close up to the window, looking over the china dogs which also looked out into the road. On days of rain or snow, in hot summer sunshine and when the pavements were covered with leaves, Richard saw the old lady, whose name he never knew.

On a bright spring morning, going back to school after the Easter break, Richard swung his bag and hummed to himself as he hurried along. Passing the thick hedge before the old lady's house, he stopped. The curtains at her window were all drawn and the house looked still and silent. Richard gazed at the window; it looked so unusual, so strange not to see her sitting there.

All through the day he thought about the drawn curtains and wondered what it could mean. In the afternoon, going home, he turned the corner and saw that the curtains were open. As he came nearer to the house, he could see that she was not there and, stopping to look in, he saw that the chair with the dark red cushion was pushed back against the wall and that the room was empty. Only the china dogs gazed back at him from the windowsill with their round, unseeing eyes.

Tears

Almighty God, Father of all mankind, in your Son you took upon yourself the world's sorrow.
We offer you our own sorrow and sadness knowing that you can help us to bear our grief through the infinite understanding and love of Jesus Christ our Lord.

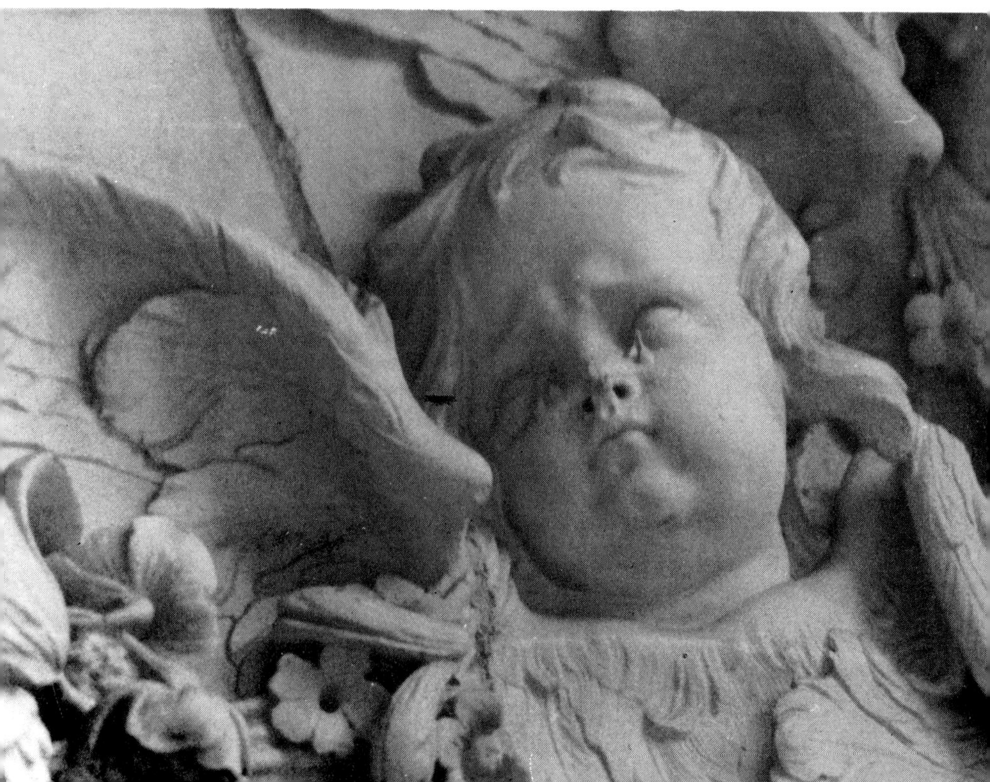

Station 5

Looking towards the High Altar

On the table which you see here is celebrated the Holy Communion, or the Lord's Supper. This is done in obedience to the command of Jesus who, on the last night of his life, had a special meal with his disciples and told them that when he had left them they were to do the same in remembrance of him. Through the ages since then, Christian people have met together at a table to remember Jesus and to share bread and wine in His presence.

Carving on the High Altar

PICTURE THIS DOME

Picture this church
as a huge triangle
balanced on a point.
At the point
you will find
two or three people
breaking bread and drinking wine
like Jesus did,
worshipping God their Father
and then
giving their lives in love
to the service of the world.

STRENGTH OF GOD

Strength of God, empower me
Love of God, enfold me
Power of God, surround me
Grace of God, protect me.

HOUSE OF GOD

This is the house of God.
But where are the rooms
To live in, to cook in, to sleep in?
No curtains to shut out the dark,
No fireplace to gather round,
No television to watch together.
What kind of house is this?

But this is the house of God.
How high the ceiling is,
How cold the unpapered walls.
No armchairs, but seats of wood,
No magazines, but books of prayers.
And it is very, very quiet,
Not like a house at all.

And yet, this is the house of God,
Where people come on Sundays
And a man talks for a long time.
Why do they call it a house?
The only thing that I can see
Which other houses always have,
Is what must be God's table.

CONVERSATION

"This place should be filled with balloons."

"Pardon?"

"I said, 'this place should be filled with balloons.' Hundreds of them. Thousands of them. Red, yellow, white and blue, floating silently and beautifully all through the building."

"Why?"

"Because this place was built for a party and no-one seems to know."

Station 6

At the memorial to John Howard

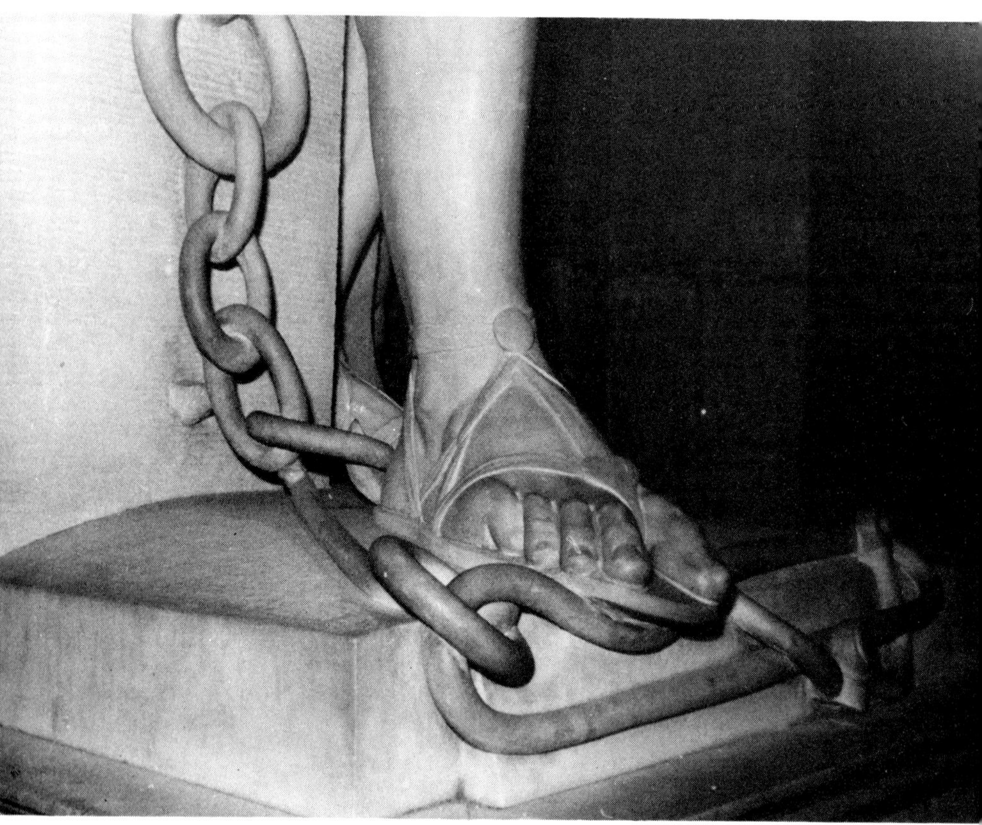

Prisons can be very bad places. John Howard spent his life trying to make them better. All over the world at this moment many people are in prison. Some of them are shut away because they have done bad things and some because they have done nothing wrong at all. As you walk freely about this Cathedral remember those whose freedom has been taken from them.

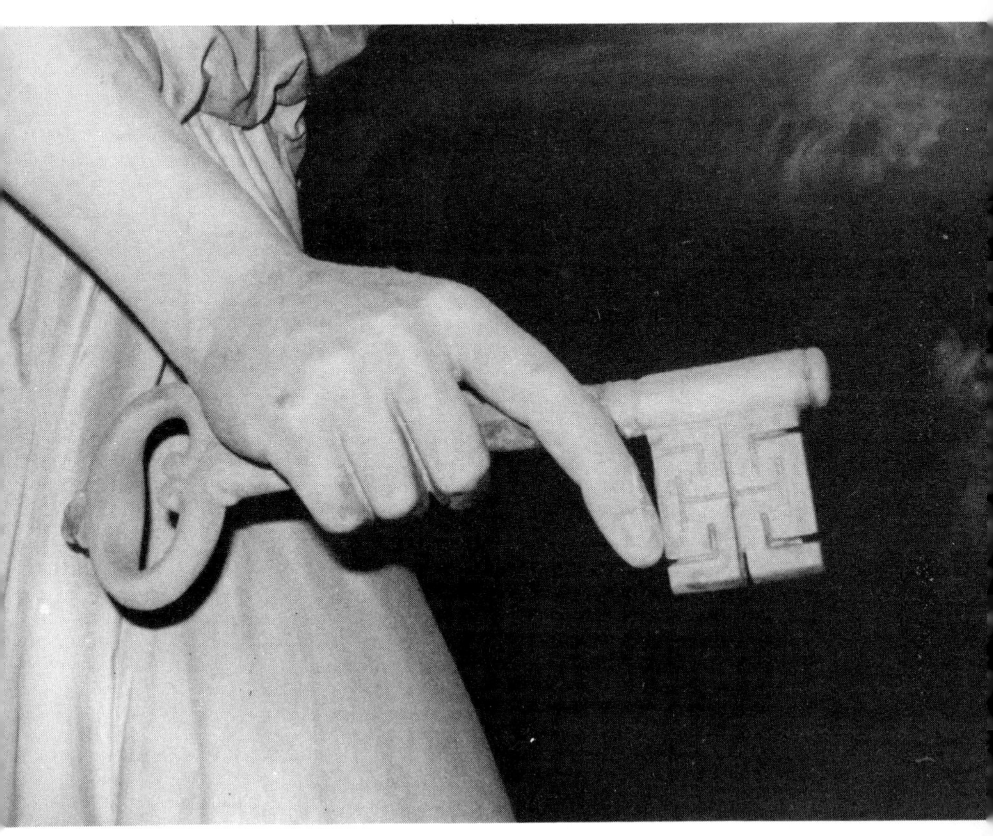

PRISONS

Lord, you are with all those in prison
sharing their boredom, their anguish,
their pleasures.
Help us to take thought for all prisoners
and not ignore them when they return to
the community.

PEACE

Father, write your peace in our hearts that we may speak peace to men for Jesus' sake.

Between the domes

CIRCLES

A circle can be so strong and forbidding. It's fine for those inside, but for those outside, it's not so good.

May our circles of friends always be open to the needs of others so that we may be generous and not mean, thoughtful and not spiteful, for Jesus' sake.

MOUSE PARABLE

"You see" said the father mouse talking to his children in a dark corner of the crypt, "some of our ancestors said that there is a great room above us and above that a glorious dome and above that a blue thing called the sky, but I want to warn you about such nonsense. It can not be true ..."

"Why not?" asked one of the children. "I sometimes hear footsteps above my head. It sounds as though there is a room over us."

"That's your imagination," said the father mouse.

"But what about the stairs - they must lead somewhere ...?"

"They are put there to tempt you," said the father. "The last time any one of our family tried venturing up the stairs he was found dead. His neck broke at the very first step."

"Surely this crypt can not be the entire world, all that there is ...?"

"Of course it is," said the father mouse. "We have everything here that we need; food, warmth, water .... would the Great Mouse need to give us anything more?"

"Just suppose," said the youngest mouse; "Just suppose one of us climbed the stairs and discovered the room and the dome and the thing called 'sky' and then came back and told you. What then?"

"I should not believe him," said the father.

"Why not?"

"Because the room and the dome and the thing called 'sky' are not there ....."

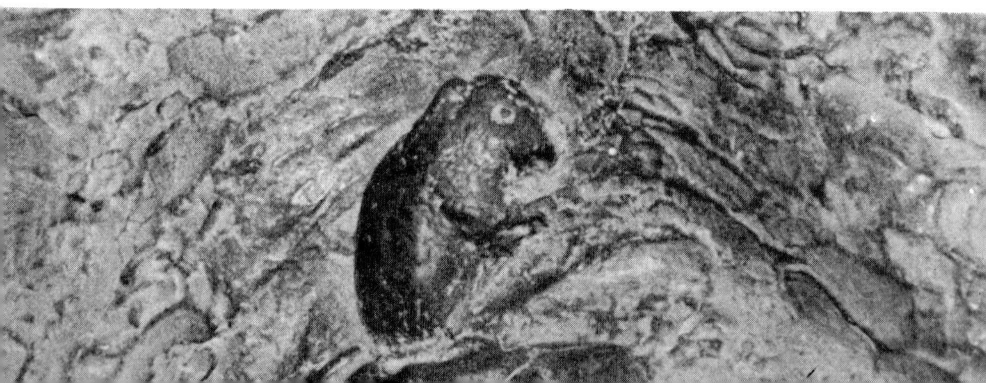

QUIETNESS

Quietness is difficult to recognise.
I think I saw it once
in the dark brown eyes
of an old and dying woman.

One of the Cathedral masons at work

The Cathedral Carver at work

Station 7

Standing by one of the large pillars which support the dome.

Under the Dome

This building encloses space. This particular space contains the pulpit, from which sermons are preached and the lectern at which readings from the Bible take place in the services. It also contains the choir, where the clergy and the men and boys gather to sing the services. The boys in the choir have their own school which is just outside the Cathedral. All of this space is enclosed in stone, mostly Portland stone from Dorset. Look at the stone, the glass and the other materials of which the building is made.

VISTAS

With a Friend in St. Paul's.

Too high these quarried walls
For us to touch,
Too hard the floors
To roll about on.
But lots of room
To explore with you.

Too many rows of chairs
Taking up space,
Too many tourists
Wandering around.
But funny things
To find with you.

Too much long history
In this great church,
Too many dead people
All around us.
But many dreams
To share with you.

Too shy to speak of love
For you, my friend,
Too grown up now,
To hold your hand.
But not too old
To giggle here with you.

SUN, DO NOT MOVE

Sun, do not move today,
Stay just where you are,
Just left of that big chimney.
Shadows do not move
Or grow darker.
Let light stay today
Just as it is.
Making the desk's wood, gold
And the white pages dazzle.
Go on warming the back of my hand
And never grow cold.
Sun, do not move today,
Stay just where you are.

SPACE

Light years separate the stars
And black holes lurk around.
Comets, planets, other worlds
All inhabit endless space.

A door closes in my mind
When I observe the universe,
Curtains drawn across my thoughts
As I consider endless space.

Our country seen from satellites
Proves the atlas to be true,
A fragment in a drop of water
Seen from endless space.

London in the south-east corner
Of this crooked little island,
Contains a church whose distances
Look like endless space.

This Cathedral called St. Paul's,
A city in a city built,
May unlock my mind to find
The end of endless space.

LIKE AN EAGLE

Like an eagle gliding upon the rising air,
Uphold me with your love, O Lord.

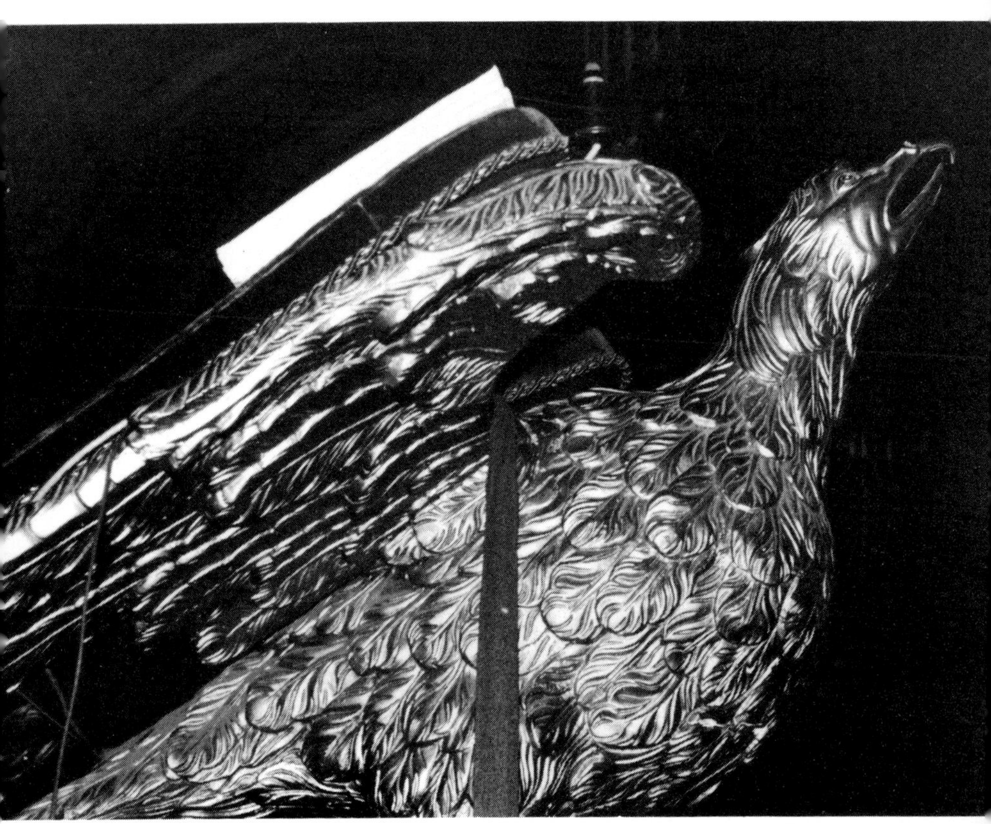

The Lectern

IN THIS SPACE

In this space, dear God, let me find the peace that I long for.

Station 8

Looking along the Nave from the West End

At the end of this long nave, at the east, you can see the High Altar. The Cathedral is built in the shape of a cross, a great cross lying in the heart of London. We can all be alone; by ourselves, in a crowd or in a great Cathedral. Looking along this nave makes us feel very small and aware of ourselves.

OPEN BUILDINGS

This building is open for me to explore.
God explores me.

This building is a place of great comfort.
God comforts me.

This building is a place of peace.
God quietens me.

This church is a place for love.
God loves me.

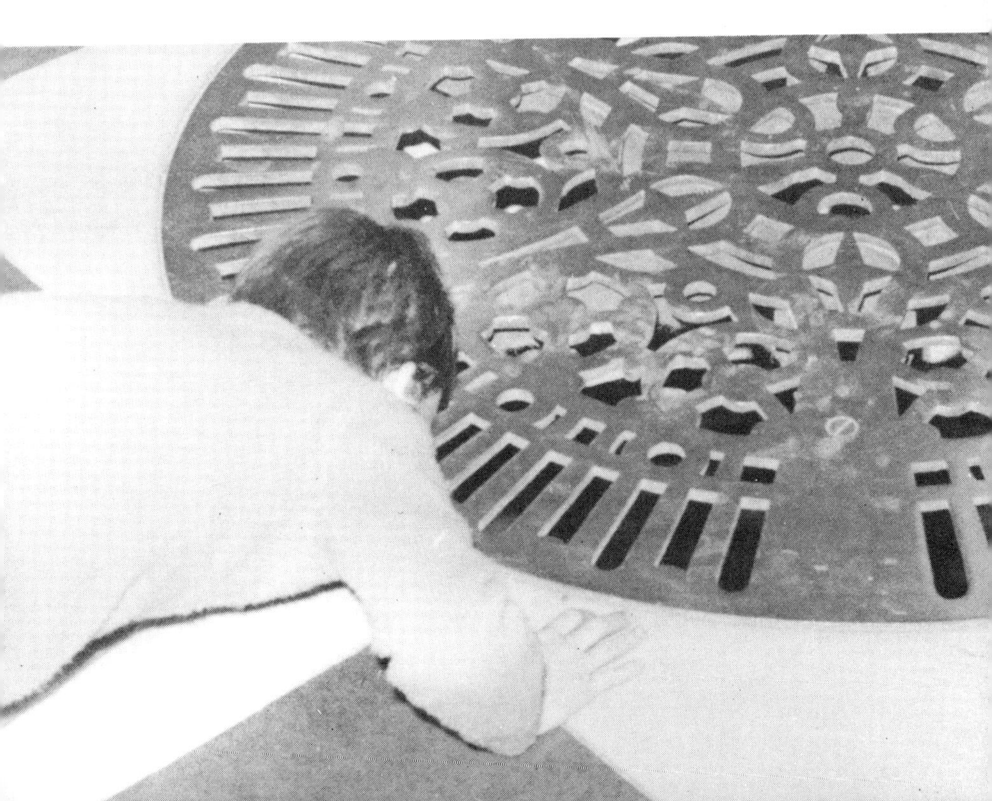

A SPLASH OF COLOUR

O Lord, save me from being a dull grey person
and let the colours of your creation
pattern my life with your beauty.

THE WONDER OF IT ALL

I should like to touch
the silence of the universe
and listen, with joy,
to the music of the sunrise.
I should like to see
the sound of the trumpet
and to taste upon my tongue
the colours of the rainbow.
I should like to smell
the waterfalls of starlight,
then dance a quiet song
for the wonder of it all.

Station 9

By the Tomb of the Duke of Wellington

In 1852 the State Funeral of the Duke of Wellington took place and he is buried in this crypt. On this crypt stands the whole weight of this huge cathedral. We feel the weight of all the wars which have been fought as we look at the memorials to those who were great soldiers. We also remember all the many men and women who died in war, but have no memorials here.

MEMORIALS

You are more than life-size
Great men of stone.
In this vast game of statues
All of you are winners.
Only when the fashion changes
Will you be moved.

These are the signs of fame;
To be turned to marble,
Frozen where no thaw can come,
Caught in continued death
With angels, whose feathered wings
Are hard and cold.

We who are small and warm,
Who breathe and move,
Give you a moment of our time,
Then turn our living backs
On you noble, famous, massive men
And go our way.

FRAGMENT FROM THE WAR

Whilst you stand here
imagining the roar of cannon
and the screams of dying men,
in a country lane
flanked by dusty, close-cropped hedges
a cat sits,
eyeing
with swishing tail
the soft brown body of a field mouse in the grass.

THE SUFFERING

Dearest, dearest God, open my heart to the
sufferings of others; fill me with your
most holy compassion that my life may be of
some help to them for Jesus' sake.

YESTERDAY, TODAY AND .....

Yesterday I saw a seed,
Today I saw a flower,
Tomorrow then will tell of death,
And I shall be no more.

DRUMS

Sitting in a meadow on a fine spring day
you hear the sound of drums - far off.
The beat is quiet, pulsating, strong,
Mixed with the rhythm of the drums comes
the noise of shouting.
Are they the drums of war
or drums for dancing?

Lord, help us to transform the war drums
into the dancing rhythm of peace.

Station 10

In the Crypt by the Tomb of Admiral Lord Nelson.

You are standing in the centre of the crypt, directly beneath the dome. This is the basement of the Cathedral, where many great people are buried, among them Lord Nelson who died at the battle of Trafalgar in 1805. Basements are where servants used to work and there are many ways of serving one another. The people remembered by their memorials in this crypt served God, their country and one another. You will find that, as well as soldiers and statesmen, artists, writers and musicians have their memorials here.

HEROES

There is something about mankind
that needs heroes
Strange and giant men
striding out towards
the very edge of things.

We step with shy precision
in their footsteps
and peer around us at the landscapes
they explored.

and are amazed
and shamed
by their audacity.

ON THE GREAT SEAS OF OUR WORLD

Father,
on the great seas of our world
ships make their way to harbour
Protect those who sail
In times of danger strengthen them
In times of peace sustain them
and give them always
the lively awareness of your unending love.

'They that go down to the sea in ships and
occupy their business in great waters
These men see the works of the Lord;
and his wonders in the deep'

O God be with them.

WHO ARE THEY?

Men with carts and brooms
Or on the back of refuse vans.
Ladies that scrub the steps
And clean the offices.

Old men mending bicycles,
Digging other people's gardens.
Delivering the morning milk,
Sweeping up the leaves.

Teachers with their patience
And nurses with gentle hands.
Shopkeepers who smile,
Policemen who grin,
Postmen who whistle.

All who do their jobs
With care and cheerfulness.
Who clean, repair, restore
More than they know
These are ministers.

JESUS

Father,

You have given us in Jesus
a light in the darkness.

May we, coming close to him,
reflect his glory
and illuminate the world with
his love.

MOMENT

Deep dark shadows
on the face of a man
contemplating God
in prayer.

The Nave, looking down from the Whispering Gallery

Station 11

Standing in the Whispering Gallery

Far below you can see tiny people walking about and when you go further up, and outside, you will look down on the buildings of London. The top of this dome is 111 metres high and the whole dome, with its eight supporting pillars, weighs about 65,000,000 kilos. Look at the paintings of the story of St. Paul, after whom this Cathedral is named. Most of our life is spent in looking up at people, but sometimes we can look down .....

LIKE A FAST, FIERCE HORSE

Take me upon your back, O God, like a fast fierce horse, then shall I exult in your strength and proclaim your power in the world.

THE POOR

We hold up to you God all the poor on the earth.
May we who are rich share our wealth,
we who are well-fed our food,
we who are educated our learning,
so that in our own small way we may contribute to
the coming of your kingdom.

AMBITION

Yes, I want to be rich,
Handsome and important.
Buy what I please,
Spend what I will
Of what is only mine.

Yes, I want to be clever,
Pass all the exams,
Come top in everything,
Know all the answers,
Always understand.

Yes, I want to be in charge,
Be strong and give the orders.
Men should salute
And stand up straight,
Whenever I appear.

Yes, I want to be loved
For my wealth, intelligence,
Position and power.
For these are me
And I am lost.

SUPPOSE

Suppose the stone
Should return again
To the earth
From where it came?

Suppose the glass
And iron should melt
And run away,
Formless once more?

Suppose the music
And all the words
Fell silent
On the still air?

Suppose this church
Should disappear,
Its great design
Become a memory?

Suppose that God
Should love the lost,
And from a ruin
Build a city?

Station 12

Standing at the Exit from the Cathedral

In the south aisle

Your mind is filled with all that you have seen, thought and imagined while you have been in this Cathedral. You can go on thinking about it and one day come back again to explore, with eyes and heart, this House of God.

THROUGH DOORS

Kenneth sat in the dentist's waiting room. The dull ache on the left side of his face, just below his ear, seemed to have gone altogether. He waggled his jaw from side to side, there was no pain at all.

"Mum", he said, "it doesn't ache any more". His mother did not look up from the magazine she was reading. "It's got to come out, Kenneth, you know it has. It won't be long now."

Kenneth looked away from his mother's face and across to the man who was waiting, arms folded and legs stretched out in front, crossed at his ankles. The man was gazing somewhere up above Kenneth's head and occasionally pursed his lips and made a short whistling sound. "I wonder if he's scared?" thought Kenneth. He didn't look it. He might as well have been waiting for a haircut with his rather bored and faraway expression on his face. "I wonder if I look scared? I bet I do."

The door opened and the lady in white smiled across at the man. "We're ready for you now", she said. Without changing his expression the man got up and walked into the dentist's room. The door closed behind him.

There was silence, broken only by the distant sound of traffic outside and a fly buzzing in one of the windows. Kenneth and his mother waited. Waited in the waiting room. Kenneth thought now that it wasn't a bit like waiting for the school bus, or for play-time to come. Not a bit like waiting for the T.V. programme or for his best friend to call. This was waiting for something he didn't want to happen. It didn't seem right, waiting for something unpleasant. Waiting to go through that door to sit in the dentist's chair. Kenneth shuddered as he thought of it.

Going through doors was funny too. Some you wanted to go through and some you didn't. He thought of all the different doors he went through, all leading from one place to another. Sometimes you went through a door to something nice and sometimes to something worse.

The door opened and the man came out, walking quickly through the waiting room and out into the street, closing the door quietly behind him. The door into the dentist's room stayed open. "Soon", thought Kenneth, "that door will close and I shall be on the other side of it."

GOD'S ELEMENTAL PRAYER

If you could hear me sing;
it would be of such intensity and glory
that the waters of the earth
would shout aloud their praise
and magnify my name.

If you could see me dance,
it would be of such graciousness and beauty
that the stones of the earth
would cry out in wonder
at such audacious skill.

If you could see me fly,
it would be of such simplicity and passion
that the very air itself
would twist around and spiral
in an ecstasy of joy.

If you could hear me pray,
it would be of such tenderness and longing
that all the fires on earth
would race up to heaven
leaving stars in their train.

LISTENING TO THE STONES

I pressed my ear to the stones of a Cathedral
and listened with terror to the sounds I heard,
the crying of a miner deep underground,
the song of a blackbird at the edge of a wood,
the gulping croak of a drowning sailor,
the roar of a crowd acclaiming their king,
the dying whispers of a soldier in a battle,
and the glorious music of a church at prayer.

KEY TO THE PHOTOGRAPHS

THE AUTHORS:

The Revd. John Hencher

Before ordination he had a career in the theatre. He has had experience as a parish priest in Worcestershire, and has taught extensively in primary schools. He was a member of the Hereford Diocesan Education Team, and is now teaching at the Bishop of Hereford's Bluecoat School.

The Revd. Christopher Herbert

Having served a curacy in Hereford where he also taught at a secondary school and ran youth clubs, he was a member of the Hereford Diocesan Education Team, and Director of Education. He is now Vicar of St. Thomas-on-the-Bourne, Farnham.

The Revd. Andrew Talbot-Ponsonby

After serving curacies in Hertfordshire and Salisbury, he became a member of the Hereford Diocesan Education Team, and had care of a group of parishes in Shropshire. He is now Vicar of Kimbolton and a group of country parishes in Herefordshire.

Previous publications include: **A PLACE TO DREAM** (1976) (C.I.O.)

Photographs taken by kind permission of the Dean and Chapter of St. Paul's Cathedral

The Authors are grateful for the support and encouragement of the Friends of St. Paul's. (The Chapter House, St. Paul's Churchyard, London, EC4M 8AD)

I S B N No. 0 902566 01 6

Set in Univers Type faces

Cover designed by A. P. Hendry

Printed by
ORPHANS PRESS LTD.,
Hereford Road, Leominster, Herefordshire, England
Tel. 2460.